THE FORGOTTEN
CHARACTERS OF
OLD SAN FRANCISCO

EMPEROR NORTON

ROBERT ERNEST COWAN, ANNE BANCROFT,
AND ADDIE L. BALLOU

THE FORGOTTEN
CHARACTERS
OF OLD
SAN FRANCISCO

Including

THE FAMOUS BUMMER & LAZARUS
AND EMPEROR NORTON

THE WARD RITCHIE PRESS

FOREWORD

The spectacular beauty of the hills and the bay of San Francisco was bypassed for a couple of centuries by the early navigators of the west coast of North America. A blanket of fog protected it from the prying eyes of both the Spanish and English whose ships crept by it in the sixteenth and seventeenth centuries. Even after it had been discovered by overland explorers it was secondary in importance to the lesser bay of Monterey, several leagues to the south of it.

The year of 1848 made the difference. With the discovery of gold in California, San Francisco with its great bay and its easy access to the gold country up the Sacramento river was the port every gold digger sought, and they came from all sides of the earth to vie and struggle for the wealth that was in the hills of the Mother Lode. There was a conglomeration of peoples who came by sea and overland to these shores. Greed, hardship and sickness took a great toll. There were thefts and murders and hangings, but there was also the great gift that man can give to man of compassion and friendship when they are apart and lonely.

San Francisco matured rapidly after the raucus first years of the gold rush. Many who had come to California in avaricious haste for gold found that there was a greater fortune in the land, and they loved it. Others, who had come as authors and journalists, were eager to write about this new and exciting part of the earth. There were also derelicts who had been unable to compete and win. Most of these sank and disappeared, but a few were enveloped in the sympathetic heart of San Franciscans and adopted

[v]

by an eager and imaginative press. In the 1860's and 1870's these latter became "The Characters of San Francisco" known and good-naturedly cherished by its citizens.

Robert Ernest Cowan, of all men I have known, knew and remembered best these interesting and fascinating characters. His memory was indelible and from the day in 1870 as a boy of eight years when he arrived in California on the recently completed transcontinental railway he forgot very little of what interested him in the new state that was to be his home for the remainder of his long life.

As the train pulled in, after the trip with his family from Canada, young Robert was greeted along with the other newcomers by Emperor Norton I in full regalia. The Emperor patted him kindly on the head, and as an old experienced head of state advised his newly arrived subject "to be a good boy."

Years later "Sir Robert," as he was affectionately called by his friends in the book circles of Los Angeles, told the story of Emperor Norton and the many other picturesque eccentrics who were in San Francisco in the 1860's and 1870's to the members of The Zamorano Club of Los Angeles. Cowan had been a bookseller in San Francisco for several decades. His infallible memory and his great interest in the history of California made him an outstanding authority on this subject. In 1914, The Book Club of California, as its first publication, issued his Bibliography of the History of California and the Pacific West, which together with the enlarged edition of 1933 compiled with his son, Robert Grannis Cowan, remains the standard bibliography of California.

In 1919, William Andrews Clark, Jr., who was then building his great library needed the help of a bibliographer and Robert E. Cowan was suggested. It proved to be a most happy association for both, with Cowan moving permanently to Los Angeles in 1926 and remaining as librarian even when after Clark's death the library became a part of the University of California at Los Angeles.

The Zamorano Club talk which Cowan gave on April 28, 1938 was much too interesting to be heard that once and forgotten, so after the meeting I suggested to "Sir Robert" that he let me print it as a keepsake for the Club members. Cowan never wrote his speeches, he never had notes, but they were precisely organized in his mind. He had an uncanny ability of selecting the exact word or expression that would give an unusual lucidity to his thoughts. His memory was such that he had no difficulty in giving me a copy almost verbatim of the talks as he had delivered it. We printed an edition of 500 copies of which 100 were bound in green wrappers and "reserved for the author and the members of the Zamorano Club" and the balance bound in boards with a cloth back for general sale. This limited number was soon exhausted and the book became one of those rare items the antiquarian book dealer so loves.

Anne Bancroft, the granddaughter of H. H. Bancroft, publisher and historian of early California, whose collection forms the basis of the Bancroft Library at the University of California at Berkeley, was one of those who acquired a copy of The Forgotten Characters of Old San Francisco. She had a special interest in two of the characters Cowan had briefly mentioned, the dogs Bummer and Lazarus, and with Cowan's encouragement completed her manuscript and submitted it to us as a companion volume to The Forgotten Characters. We liked it and issued it in a limited edition of 500 copies in a format similar to the previous book. It was published under the title of The

Memorable Lives of Bummer & Lazarus (Citizens of San Francisco) 1857-1865. *It was quickly sold out and became a collector's item.*

The third part of this book was resurrected from an early newspaper story about Emperor Norton that was called to my attention by Robert G. Cowan. It appeared in the September 28, 1908 issue of the San Francisco Sunday Call *and was written by Addie Lucia Ballou who appears to have been an extremely active and aggressive woman. She was a nurse during the Civil War before moving to San Francisco, a noted suffragette, a notary public and a portrait painter. Her paintings include U.S. Grant, George Bromley and M.H. De Young, as well as the picture of Emperor Norton which is reproduced in this book. The account which she wrote is a contemporary one from one who knew Norton very well.*

I should like to express the appreciation of The Ward Ritchie Press to those who have helped in the gathering of the material in this book. I wish to thank Robert Grannis Cowan, Anne Bancroft and the San Francisco Call-Bulletin *for permission to print the biographical material included in this book. Robert Weinstein, of our own organization, has been particularly helpful in locating and suggesting illustrative material, as have been John Barr Tompkins, head of Public Services, Bancroft Library, University of California at Berkeley; James De Tarr Abajian, Librarian, California Historical Society; Irene Simpson, Director, Wells Fargo History Room; Mrs. Helen S. Giffen, Librarian, Society of California Pioneers; the Special Collections Department, San Francisco Public Library; and the History Department of the Los Angeles County Museum.* WARD RITCHIE

February, 1964

CONTENTS

ILLUSTRATIONS

THE FORGOTTEN
CHARACTERS OF
OLD SAN FRANCISCO

MONTGOMERY STREET, SAN FRANCISCO, 1865

THE FORGOTTEN
CHARACTERS OF
OLD SAN FRANCISCO

BY ROBERT ERNEST COWAN

All cities have had that singular class of eccentric individuals commonly and generally known as "characters."
Of these San Francisco has had perhaps more than her
share. The years from 1860 to 1885 were generously pro-
lific of these freaks. Some were men of affairs—gentlemen
all, but who exhibited mild and harmless eccentricities;
some were impoverished, soiled and ragged; some were
hopelessly woebegone and pathetic; some in personal appearance were fantastic or picturesque—some even gro-
tesque; some were noted for sheer strength of character or
vitality or obsessions; others, fewer in number, were those
who retained something of the gentility of their happier

days and bore themselves with consistent and conspicuous dignity to the end.

In San Francisco in the sixties, the popular promenade was through the streets Montgomery and Kearny from Jackson to Sutter. Here in the late afternoon might be seen as in a rapidly shifting kaleidoscope, a most unusual procession, relieved here and there by the injected "characters" who lent life and color to the warp and woof of the most strangely variegated tapestry. A strange small army they were, each member living his own singular life and absorbed in his own mysterious schemes. Here were "George Washington Coombs," known also as the "Great Matrimonial Candidate;" "Old Rosey;" "Money King;" "The Great Unknown;" "The Fat Boy;" "Old Crisis," and others, all of whom long since have passed into oblivion. And in this motley throng though never of it, appeared "Emperor Norton."

Frederick Coombs, known as "George Washington" was a photographer who came to California in 1849. He bore somewhat of a resemblance to the first president, and this he accentuated by wearing a costume of the colonial period. All of the properties were correct in details. Coat, waistcoat and knee-breeches were of black velvet. The neck, bosom and wrists were adorned with fine lace. A three-cornered hat, black silk stockings, and low shoes with heavy buckles completed his outfit, and the ensemble was vividly striking. To add to this general impressiveness he sometimes carried a delicate court sword.

He also announced himself to be "The Great Matrimonial Candidate." About 1860, he opened a phrenological parlor which met with unusual success. Very soon it

"GEORGE WASHINGTON" COOMBS

was quite the proper thing for both sexes of San Francisco's elite to visit the learned and eminent Professor George Washington Coombs.

Whether this graft failed or the Professor became tired of it is not known, but about 1867 he left California. In New York, in 1869, he published a book: "The Dawn of the Millennium—One Hundred Pictorial Illustrations of some Passages in the Life and Thrilling Adventures of the Author, Pioneer, and Missionary of Science and Beneficence." It is a weird volume, and apparently written after the author's mind had become somewhat unbalanced.

Old Rosey was a mass of greasy rags, soiled and unkempt. But beneath this repellant exterior there must have been something of the aesthetic. He never appeared on parade without a flower in his ragged lapel. He seemed to have had the freedom of some flower-garden. Roses were his preference, hence the nickname. In default of a rose he sometimes wore a carnation or a sprig of heliotrope, and upon one rare occasion he sported a hyacinth.

Money King was in no sense a loafer. He was a money lender and a sort of curbstone broker. He carried a banner which bore the inscription: "Money King. You can borrow money cheap."

Beyond gross lateral displacements the "Fat Boy" had no marks of distinction. He was, simply as Falstaff termed it: a "great hulking mass of fat" which may be seen at any time in any large city.

Unlike any of these others was the "Great Unknown." He was a singularly handsome individual; tall, erect and slender. His hair was jet black, and he was clean-shaven at a time when almost every man wore a beard of generous growth. He was consistently well-groomed in the broad-cloth of that day. His top hat was well brushed, his linen was immaculate, and his boots were always resplendent with polish. (All gentlemen wore boots at that period.) He was entirely aloof and mysterious, and none had any speaking acquaintance with him. Some rumor whispered that he was an exiled nobleman, and another that he was an expatriated diplomat. One day he was missed in the afternoon parade.

His body was found in a loft near the waterfront where it appeared that he made a livelihood by stuffing pillows and mattresses. The large room was scantily furnished. His clothing and linen, still immaculate, were carefully hung over a chair, and his resplendent boots were arranged in military fashion beside the chair. On a small dressing stand a wig of jet-black hair hung over a wig-block. On the rude bed lay the body. The face a fine frozen mask as handsome in death as it had been in life, but surmounted with a heavy growth of snow-white hair. Whatever his identity and secrets had been, they went with him, and he remained the "Great Unknown" to the end.

"Old Crisis" was one J. L. Hopkins, an unfrocked clergyman, possibly of the Episcopalian faith. In the early seventies each Sabbath morning, sidewalk services in front of the old Whatcheer House were conducted by the Rev. Henry Cox, Methodist. Mr. Cox was a noted and eloquent speaker as were many others of that time. He was known as "Hallelujah" Cox, because of his oft-uttered expressions of joy. Mr. Hopkins assembled his followers on the opposite side of the street and his frequently voiced slogan was: "The crisis is at hand." Mr. Cox preached a straight, ortho-

FROM THE WASP OCT. 5, 1878

dox "go to Heaven" doctrine. Mr. Hopkins listened carefully to all of Cox's arguments and promptly refuted them by giving them a "go to Hell" twist, for he too was an orator. This afforded much entertainment to many for a couple of years, but it came to an end when Rev. Cox was called elsewhere. But "Old Crisis" had other affairs. For many years, in fact until his death in 1900, he conducted a matrimonial bureau and published a paper entitled: "The San Francisco Gossip and Matrimonial Advocate." This dubious business must have been lucrative for the quondam preacher was always well-dressed. His journal contained numerous advertisements of ladies who desired acquaintance with the object (or hope) of matrimony. Feminine pulchritude at that time must have been more universal than it is now, for all of these applicants were "beautiful, cultured and refined." Then too, the fact that individually each could contribute from $1000 to $5000 added much to the generous attractions of the dear creatures as prospective domestic partners.

It may be accepted as a postulate that no generation is ever replaced by another. It is merely a succession in which most of the earlier features of the mode of living, trend of thought, and tastes have either disappeared or have become greatly altered. By 1875, most of these strange characters had disappeared forever.

In San Francisco from 1870 to 1890, the uppermost political question was that of Chinese immigration. The opposition to the influx of the Chinese and the employment of their labor had smouldered for twenty years, but it was kept alive by some of the primitive labor unions such as the "Miners Union," and the "Knights of St. Crispin." The situation became violently inflamed in 1876. Sundry isolated Chinese wash houses and match factories were burned. Many unprovoked assaults were made upon inoffensive Chinese and several lives were lost. It was a Roman holiday greatly enjoyed by the hoodlums of the time but there were many others who participated in these grim festivities. This state of affairs continued for several months during which the government calmly sat on the side as a disinterested spectator. The climax came when the mob threatened to loot Chinatown, and openly attempted to destroy the China mail dock. Then, and then only, were the complacent authorities aroused to action. The state militia was called out, and the citizens organized the third vigilance committee of San Francisco; the Committee of Safety, more popularly known as the "Pickhandle Brigade." Out of this welter of violence and confusion there appeared Denis Kearney, independent drayman.

Kearney was a native of Ireland who had come to San Francisco about 1867. Aggressive and active, he became a powerful figure among the members of the early labor unions which presently were organized into the Workingmen's Party of California. Besides being a capable leader, he was a natural orator of considerable ability and rude eloquence. His rhetoric was a bit fragile in spots, but this never disturbed his audiences. Nightly, for several years, he hippodromed his audience on the sand-lots which are now the civic center. He gave the people exactly what they liked to hear, and his following was a large one. Under flaring torches from a rough platform, he vehemently pronounced anathema upon the Chinese and all their works,

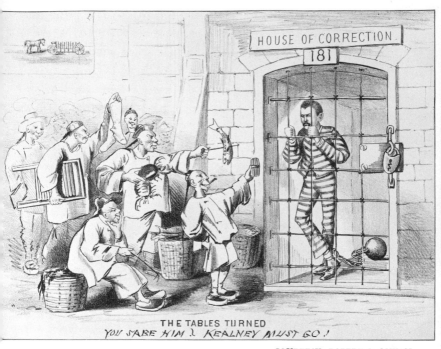

THE TABLES TURNED

YOU SABE HIM! KEALNEY MUST GO!

TABLES TURNED

and each oration was ended by the famous slogan: "The Chinese must go!" Occasionally, as a diversion, he blasted the magnates who lived in luxury on Nob hill. His parting slogan in these speeches was the sinister and significant one of: "Hemp! Hemp! Hemp!"

The patience of the civic authorities either became exhausted or some pressure was brought to arouse them from their lethargy. Kearney had previously been arrested but in 1880, charges of inciting riots and disturbing the peace were successfully brought against him and he was sequestrated in the county jail. The Workingmen's Party had elected the Rev. Isaacs S. Kalloch as mayor of San Francisco and the spectacular sequences of his stormy career were before the public actively for a couple of years. In this interval the excitement of the Chinese question had somewhat subsided. Then too, Kearney doubtless had time for reflection during his term in duress vile. He returned to his dray and the sand-lot knew him no more. Later, he opened an employment bureau which was continued until 1906.

Another leading exponent of the Chinese question was Dr. Charles Carroll O'Donnell. He claimed that he was a lineal descendant of Charles Carroll of Virginia, and that statement was never disputed. He was a specialist with a large and active practice. He too was strongly moved by the presence of the many Chinese in San Francisco. His office was at Kearny and Washington streets facing Portsmouth Square. He was an orator of considerable ability and from the balcony of his office he delivered many forceful addresses. It was his custom to have these printed in broadside form and a few such are yet extant. Later he published a paper called *The Anti-Coolie Thunderbolt*.

It was one of the weirdest papers ever issued in California. O'Donnell at that time was making a brave attempt to become governor of California. The journal contained current accounts of the progress of his campaign and its platforms, interspersed with fierce editorials concerning the dreadful evils of the local Chinese and their awful menace to society. It was embellished with frightful cartoons exhibiting the sinister activities of the Mongolian colony. The favorite themes were: Chinese lotteries; opium-smoking; prostitution; the Chinese avocations of house-servants, laundrymen and shoemakers. Another choice topic for frequent discussion was leprosy, and this was always profusely and hideously illustrated. It was the unique product of a unique time.

The militant doctor cherished political ambitions and aspired to be coroner of San Francisco. As an independent candidate he met with defeats upon two occasions but finally he was elected. Whatever may have been his limitations in other directions, he proved to be throughout his term of office one of the most capable and efficient coroners that the city has had. When he assumed office he instituted sundry drastic reforms, some of which are yet active.

Another odd contemporary was John Vincent, "The Razor Man." He had a portable stand nightly at Pine and Kearny streets. It was a source of amusement for children. A series of carved wooden, movable figures worked by a foot-treadle represented the operations of turning a grindstone, sharpening a razor and the like. He also had a strong antipathy for the Chinese and gave utterance to it in a pamphlet entitled: *Our Boys*, wherein he earnestly coun-

THE PROMENADE

selled the white boys of San Francisco to avoid the Chinese devils and all of their works. Some of the older residents of San Francisco can yet remember Vincent croaking hoarsely: "Get your razor ground!"

During the eighties there were two individuals who came briefly under the glare of the calcium lights. "Oofty-Goofty," whose proper name was Marks, was a Hebrew of dubious antecedents. Except in a monkeyish way he never was a crook. He lived mostly by his wits and as they were not of a very superior order his living was not luxurious. For ten days he had lent himself to a sideshow on Market street. There, in a cage, he was billed as a "Wild Man." His duties were to scowl and grimace and at intervals to beat his breast and roar: "Oofty-Goofty." He was reasonably successful, but unhappily it was in the heat of summer and the thick fur which had been glued to his body was too dense to permit perspiration and quite naturally he became ill. He was put into a tub of hot water. Some of the fur came away but also considerable human integument. Some inspired idiot conceived the bright scheme of exposing him to the sun that the tarry glue might be melted. Again success was only partial. More fur came off, but much more of poor Oofty's skin came with it. Ultimately he recovered, but he probably retained some patches of that fur so long as he lived.

Once, under the conditions of a wager, Oofty was put in a packing-box and shipped as ordinary freight to Sacramento. His reward was to be $10.00. He had food and water and the case was ventilated of course, but it was painfully small. The baggage-smashers performed their parts in perfect sangfroid. When the freight arrived, Oofty was a pitiful mass of bumps and bruises but they were assuaged somewhat by the ten dollars which he collected.

On one occasion he was knocked down by a vehicle and being seriously injured was placed in a hospital. Sometime after his recovery he made the discovery that a certain portion of his anatomy was devoid of sensation. This gave him an idea which, with monkeyish cunning, he proceeded to capitalize. He carried a baseball bat or a sawed-off billiard cue wherever he went. For the modest amount of fifty cents he would stoop and permit any interested individual to strike him with the club. Force, gentle or crushing was alike to the apathetic Oofty, and he garnered many four-bit pieces. The end came however, when one day a stranger lifted and applied the club. Oofty went down in dire defeat and remained out for a couple of hours. He said later that after that crushing experience he was never the same man. Oofty's adherence to truth wavered at times but in this instance it was never questioned. The illustrious stranger who valiantly swung the bat was John L. Sullivan.

"Big Bertha the Confidence Queen" was Mrs. Bertha Stanley of New York. The delicate allusion to her size was earned by the fact that she was a large and voluminous person who weighed 300 pounds on the hoof, so to speak. Her graft was promise of marriage for cash and she had been moderately successful. Among other operations, she had relieved one New York gentleman of $25,000. Whether New York became too torrid; whether her graft had played out; or whether Inspector Byrnes had conveyed some delicate hint that she shift her freight is not known, but in the middle eighties she appeared in San Francisco.

At that time San Francisco was the mecca for the delegates of all of the unholy fraternities in Christendom. Latterly, the mantle has fallen upon Los Angeles where the field is broader, wealth more superlative, and credulity is greater.

Jack Hallinan, clever showman and theatrical manager, was proprietor of a theatre on the far-famed Barbary Coast. He retained Big Bertha to perform in tights as "Mazeppa." For a couple of nights the act was successful and the fiery, untamed steed performed his part perfectly. Then came a debacle. The horse may have taken fright or he may have mistook his cue. More probably he balked at the heavy load he was carrying. He and "Big Bertha" backed over the footlights into the orchestra with appalling results. The tuba was flattened out; the bass fiddle was demolished; and the orchestra was completely demoralized.

Hallinan was a heroic soul and he was undaunted. He also was proprietor of another similar theatre on Market street. It too was of somewhat low social and moral degree, and just shortly before it had been released from an injunction placed upon it by the police. Presently Hallinan retained as performer the near-skeleton, Oofty, and the expansive Bertha. The act was a burlesque of the Balcony Scene from Romeo and Juliet. On the stage in mediaeval costume, Oofty declaimed in impassioned accents, and from the balcony, Big Bertha in tights coyly responded. It was an edifying spectacle. Mindful of that earlier disaster, Hallinan took no unnecessary chances. He had props put under the stage, and the balcony was constructed of 4x6 timbers.

The quaint and unusual characters were fast disappearing from San Francisco. The fantastic and picturesque of the earlier days were gone forever. Those who had been briefly conspicuous through unusual avocations or intense principles had retired to a more normal and less exciting mode of living. The lurid and rococo gentry had moved on to fresh fields for exploitation. The old order of men and things had passed away.

There were a few individuals of personality whose fads and foibles set them apart from the general rank and file. They were in no sense public characters. They were gentlemen all, men of affairs and excellent social standing. Three of them were members of the Bohemian Club and all are remembered with affection by the many who knew them. An anecdote concerning each is sufficient to characterize them.

Philo Jacoby was editor of *The Hebrew* which he established during the Civil War. He was also champion rifle shot of the world. At the Centennial Exposition in Philadelphia in 1876, there was held an international rifle shooting match. There had been in the many competing countries, 20,000 contestants. In the final eliminations two hundred of the world's most expert marksmen were assembled in Philadelphia, and Philo Jacoby of San Francisco won the coveted title of: "Champion Rifle Shot of the World." He was one of the early members of the Olympic Club an athlete of great prowess for which, together with his superb marksmanship, he had received a great number of medals and trophies. In civic parades, seated in a carriage, his was a familiar figure and his breast was

COURTESY: CALIF. HIST. SOCIETY

PHILO JACOBY

covered with medals. Modestly he said that he wore only a third of his well-earned decorations.

During the Civil War, a certain country town editor had written an editorial in which President Lincoln was rather severely criticized. This greatly offended Jacoby and in *The Hebrew* he made a very blunt and drastic reply. The country editor was thoroughly angered and he made the threat that the next time that he was in San Francisco he would hunt out that "bullet-headed little Jew" and horsewhip him. Presently he came to San Francisco and being entertained by a friend he was taken to an exhibition given by the Olympic Club. On the platform a heavyset, black-bearded little man twisted horseshoes, calmly bent a crowbar, and cracked cobblestones with his hand. When the pyramid was formed, he as the apex, fanned out six men. The country editor was profoundly impressed. "Wonderful," he said. "Most extraordinary! I never imagined that one man could possess such enormous strength. Who is that little man?" And his friend replied, sotto voce: "That's the bullet-headed little Jew whom you are intending to horsewhip." The country editor quietly returned to the safety of his remote sanctum and the threatened castigation was forgotten.

Samuel M. Brookes was an artist and his studies of still life were the finest that have ever been made in California. Much of his work was lost in the fire of 1906, but some examples of his skill are yet to be seen in a few of the older residences and art galleries. He moved into the old Studio building on Clay street and occupied a room on the third floor. Among his effects was a worn and discarded smock which, artist-like he carelessly threw over what he thought was a hook on the wall. He found no running water in his studio, and the general supply was in the basement. For a number of years he laboriously trudged up and down three flights of stairs four times daily, carrying his bucket of water. When he finally moved out, the old smock was taken along with the rest of his belongings. Then he was cruelly scandalized to discover that the "hook" was a faucet containing running water.

The sole idiosyncracy of Laurie Bunten was mild and entirely harmless. He was a Scotchman, courteous and affable and a popular member of the Bohemian club. A finely characteristic cartoon of him made by a gifted member may yet be seen in one of the rooms of the club. His bete-noir was the abbreviation of his name, which he insisted should be fully written: "Mr. Laurie Bunten" and not "L. Bunten." At that time the club was on Post street over Alexander Robertson's bookshop. Here for reasons of his own, Mr. Bunten had all his mail delivered and periodically he would call for it. It was in the care of a young lady clerk who was accustomed to tie it up and inscribe it "Mr. L. Bunten." She had been gently admonished upon two or three occasions but the day came for her final lesson in that feature of social usage. As usual, the packet bore the abhored superscription: "Mr. L. Bunten."

"Young woman," said Mr. Bunten in fine Scotch accents: "When you address your Maker do you say J. Christ or Jesus Christ?" My name is Mr. Laurie Bunten and not L. Bunten." The wholesome lesson was learned and the young lady never again committed the same transgression.

In a very different way Henry Heyman also was mind-

COURTESY: ROBERT G. COWAN

SIR HENRY HEYMAN

ful of the shadow of a great name. Violinist, born in San Francisco in 1854, he had received his musical training at one of the great conservatories in Germany. He was not a great violinist but he was a very excellent teacher. In the middle eighties he went to the Sandwich Islands where he became court violinist to King Kalakaua. Upon his return to San Francisco he announced himself as Sir Henry Heyman. His cards, social and professional, all bore "Sir Henry Heyman," and when acquaintances inadvertently omitted the title, they were quietly but promptly reminded of their discourtesy. In the regal days of the Islands there was an order of knighthood known as the "Star of Oceania," so there is no question of Sir Henry's claims and titular rights. But a clever, graceless member of the club placed a different and rather irreverant construction upon it. He said that one evening when Kalakaua was in the salon he called for music and Sir Henry dutifully played upon his violin. The King's patience at best was not long suffering. He endured the music so long as he could and then he exclaimed: "Good night!", and thus was Sir Henry knighted.

Four men, all prominent and well known San Franciscans were especially conspicuous for their common choice in style of headgear. They were familiar figures about town and known to many hundreds of its residents. Dr. William F. McNutt, and Dr. Charles P. Chesley, both prominent; Alvinza Hayward, capitalist; and Isidor N. Choynski, bookseller and editor of *Public Opinion*. The preference was for a high black stovepipe hat. This was nothing unusual for tophats were extensively worn at that time. But when the brim was ironed out flat (which was the fancy of these four gentlemen) the general effect was somewhat striking.

In later years, but before 1906, three well-remembered street characters were blind. Mr. Bates the lavender vendor was not in any sense a mendicant and he was always decently and carefully dressed. The other two were street beggars. One was a tall Indian who played on the harmonica; the other a German whose alms-receptacle was a cigar box tied to his waist with a piece of hay rope. A highly entertaining tale of an encounter of these three worthies was written in his inimitable style by Frank Norris in his book entitled: "The Third Circle."

During those colorful years there were sundry others whose tangential careers set them apart from their fellow kind, but who have become legendary. Almost completely forgotten are the names of: "Philosopher Pickett," able journalist and lawyer who consistently fought from the other side; "White-Hat McCarthy" who late in life realized his ambition to sport a white beaver hat; "Schonchin Maloney," politician loud with jawbone, but otherwise negligible; "Father Elphick," the news vendor and vegetarian; Godfrey Diamond, the "Apostle of longevity," who lived up to his doctrines and died at the noble age of 114 years; and Major Michael Hawkins, courteous and affable, once known as the "Beau Brummel of San Francisco."

"Emperor Norton" was the noblest and best known of all of the strange characters of that earlier period. Joshua A. Norton was his real name. He was of Hebrew parentage, born February 4, 1819, either in Edinburgh or London. Of his early life there is little known as he rarely spoke of it. Like many others who came to California at that time,

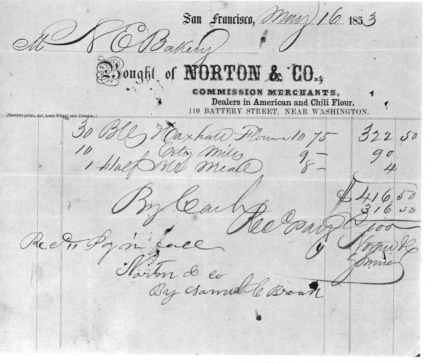

NORTON COMPANY BILL

he lived too actively in the present and the past was seldom mentioned. Before coming to California he had been for some time at Algoa Bay, Cape of Good Hope and it is said that while there he had been a member of the Cape Mounted Riflemen. He finally reached San Francisco in December, 1849, having come from Rio de Janeiro on the Hamburg vessel *Franzika*.

Norton at once engaged in business. He was occupied in extensive transactions in real estate, and many tremendous operations in importation commissions. His native shrewdness was even unusual; his intelligence was wonderfully clear, and his business judgment was remarkably accurate. To these acumen were added the rarer attributes of a sound and inflexible moral and financial integrity. Some of these commissions involved transactions to the extent of several hundreds of thousands of dollars weekly, and Joshua Norton rapidly became wealthy. He had brought with him to California, $40,000, and towards the close of 1853, he had amassed a fortune of a quarter of a million dollars.

In 1853, in association with one Thorne and others he attempted to control the rice market. Earlier he had operated heavily, had been uniformly successful, and was applauded for his daring and foresight, cooperation was offered and accepted from other large firms and an immense quantity of rice was secured and held. Everything was promising for yield of immense fortune as profit, as rice was thirty-six cents per pound in bulk unloaded. Almost the last pound of rice in this port had been purchased by the combination. The profits were being calculated when two unexpected cargoes of rice arrived, which the combination could not take up nor control. The market was drugged and prices fell much below cost. To add to the general disaster, in order to protect themselves, some of the associated firms sold out and Norton was financially ruined. He contended stoutly to his closing days that one well-known firm owed him $60,000.

Extensive litigation followed. The first of these cases was that of Ruiz Hermanos vs. Norton, et al. In this contention Norton was sustained in the lower court, but upon appeal this decision was reversed by the Supreme Court. This was in November, 1853. Other serious embarrassments followed, and the sacrifice of his extensive holdings of real estate, principally around North Beach, was the last chapter of his unfortunate disaster. The previous excitement of false expectation and shock of these disappointments, coupled with the legal troubles, constituted a severe blow to Norton's sanity. He retired into obscurity, and when he emerged in 1857, he gave palpable and distinct evidence of an overthrown mind.

His obsession took the form of a belief that he was the Emperor of the United States. He claimed that by an act of the legislature of 1853, he had been made Emperor of California. With this he was dissatisfied, and not unreasonably so, for he argued that California was but one of a union of states, and as such could neither loyally nor logically create an emperor. Furthermore, he would not renounce what he styled the "national cause," so the act was accordingly suppressed.

The earliest printed proclamation of the self-created Emperor appeared in 1859.

1st Proclamation

Norton I. Gratia Dei Emperor
US and Protector of
Mexico having full Confidence
& trust in J. Ross Browne.
Do hereby Commend his
appointment to the Court
of China & do hereby
Grant him full Authority
to act for our Imperial
Govt

Norton I.

HANDWRITTEN NORTON PROCLAMATION

At the pre-emptory request and desire of a large majority of the citizens of these United States, I, Joshua Norton, formerly of Algoa Bay, Cape of Good Hope, and now for the last 9 years and 10 months past of S. F., Cal., declare and proclaim myself Emperor of these U. S., and direct the representatives of the different States of the Union to assemble in Musical Hall, of this city, on the 1st day of Feb. next, then and there to make such alterations in the existing laws of the Union as may ameliorate the evils under which the country is laboring, and thereby cause confidence to exist, both at home and abroad, in our stability and integrity.

NORTON I.
Emperor of the United States

17th September, 1859.

Having assumed the sword and the plume, Norton I actively entered upon the many duties that pertained to his royal station. It is of interest to note that the pretensions of Norton were early recognized by the public of San Francisco and as speedily humored. His name had temporarily disappeared from the city directory, but in Langley's issue for 1862, we find the following: "Norton, Joshua (Emperor), dwl. Metropolitan Hotel." His empire was established and Norton I, Emperor of the United States had begun to reign.

One day at this period, some important news was received from Mexico, and in this as in all such matters, the Emperor was greatly interested. In a spirit of levity, some joker stated that Mexico needed a protector, and suggested that Norton was the logical choice. Thereupon "Protector of Mexico" was added to the official title and retained for almost a decade. It was dropped during the unhappy career of Maximilian, for, as Norton sanely and even prophetically observed: "It is impossible to protect such an unsettled nation."

The imperialistic duties were manifold, comprehending grave affairs both national and international. The civil war gave him deep concern. On July 12, 1860, he declared the Union dissolved. Early in the war he declared a blockade, and in 1862 he issued a mandate to the Protestant and Catholic churches to publicly ordain him as Emperor, that he might more efficiently bring order out of the chaos into which the country had been plunged by the violent conflict and fierce dissensions of its rebellious people.

Some of the proclamations to be found in the contemporary journals were jokes which originated with the graceless wags and inspired idiots of the day. Others of which one or two are extant, were the inspiration of Norton alone. They are couched in terms of sanity and composed in superior English. Most of them are national in purport and bear upon relations with Great Britain, Russia, Mexico and other foreign countries. Others relate to the affairs of the civil war. One has survived which is entirely personal. In February, 1860, the Emperor desired to visit Sacramento where the legislature was then in session. The Steam Navigation company denied him transportation. Norton issued an order to the commander of the revenue cutter to blockade the Sacramento river until the offending company could be brought to terms.

The proclamations appearing as jokes are easily to be recognized. Norton had no part in them as they were the work of the conscienceless wags and amiable villains of

PROCLAMATION.

WHEREAS, Certain parties having assumed prerogatives, pertaining only to my Royal self; AND WHEREAS, in the furtherance of such assumption, they have printed and circulated treasonable and rebellious documents, circulars, sermons and proclamations, calculated to distract and divide the allegiance of my subjects; AND WHEREAS, it has come to my knowledge that a certain seditious proclamation and command has been distributed amongst the most faithful of my agents and subjects, of which the following is a copy, to-wit:

"OFFICE WELLS, FARGO & CO.

"SAN FRANCISCO, JULY 4TH, 1868.

"TO OUR AGENTS:

"C. Averill, formerly Forwarding Clerk, and late Messenger to our Mexican Coast Offices, has left our employ and gone with the Pacific Union Express Company.

"You will treat him as any other employee of an opposition Express Co.

"CHARLES E. McLANE,

"Gen'l Agent."

NOW, THEREFORE, I, EMPEROR NORTON the First, do hereby command that no notice shall be paid to proclamations issued by Pretenders to my authority, ability, and Regal position.

AND IT IS FURTHER COMMANDED, that any violation of this command shall be reported to me, in order that I may banish the offender from my Kingdom.

NORTON, EMPEROR THE FIRST.

COURTESY: WELLS FARGO BANK

TYPICAL PRINTED PROCLAMATION FROM NORTON I

the times. One of these fictitious documents was issued in observance of the forty-sixth birthday of the Emperor:

Owing to unsettled questions between His Majesty Maximilian I, El Duque de Gwino, The Tycoon, the King of the Mosquitos, the King of the Cannibal Islands, &c., the usual display of bunting on foreign shipping and on public buildings, in commemoration of our 46th birthday, will be omitted.
Feb. 4, 1865.

Another proclamation was to the effect that the Emperor contemplated marriage, but to avoid arousing jealousy among the fairer sex, he played no favorites and they were to decide for themselves which one of them should be Empress.

Falsified telegraphic news was also a source of great amusement for the versatile wits. In 1864, Jefferson Davis telegraphed to inquire if it were true that Norton was in sympathy with Lincoln, also the request that $500 be sent, as Davis had but one pair of trousers, and even that was worn out. Another telegram was from Lincoln. The President thanked the Emperor for his support, and said he had a good story to tell but at present was too busy settling accounts with a seedy individual named Davis. Norton was instructed to proceed to Petaluma, there to remain until further official notice. What the Emperor thought of these effusions will never be known. But interlinear reading is not altogether difficult, for in many directions the mind of Norton was unusually clear, and at all times he was remarkably philosophic.

During his long reign the equanimity of the Emperor was never seriously disturbed except by the actions of two individuals.

The first of these was D. Stellifer Moulton, formerly New York correspondent of the *Boston Traveller*. In 1865, he proclaimed a monarchy and styled himself, "Stellifer the King, Reigning Prince of the House of David, and Guardian of Mexico." Stellifer was of fine education and possessed luxurious tastes, but unlike Norton, he was entirely insane. He had lived at the leading hotels in New York and Boston, and when dunned by them had agreed to pay upon receipt of his claims against the United States Treasury for $3,500,000, which was to be his semi-annual allowance. In a republic such regal ambitions are not always appreciated, so the authorities apprehended Stellifer the King, and promptly sequestered him. This state of affairs was too much for our Emperor. He, himself, was of the House of David, and also was he not Protector of Mexico? He purged his soul of its bitter resentment which flamed forth in the following:

PROCLAMATION

Down with usurpers and imposters! Off with his head! So much for cooking other people's goose! The legitimate authorities of New York are hereby commanded to seize upon the person of one Stellifer, styling himself King or Prince of the House of David, and send him in chains to San Francisco, Cal., for trial before our Imperial Court, on various charges of fraud alleged against him in the public prints.

NORTON I.

Emperor of the United States and Protector of Mexico
S. F. 6th day of Nov., 1865.

The other member of the grossly offending duo was Denis Kearney, famed for his sand-lot statesmanship and anti-Chinese oratory. For Denis, the Emperor favored

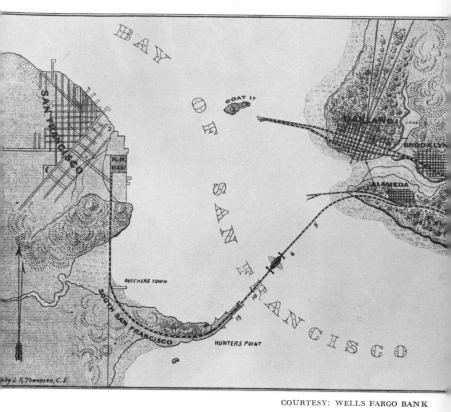

1871 PLAN FOR THE BAY BRIDGE

speedy judicial extermination. At the same time the new Constitution also exasperated and he denounced it as high treason. He would have destroyed it but was willing to have the eminent attorney, Hall McAllister legally annul it.

His most famous proclamation was issued August 18, 1869. Whether or not it was drafted by the Emperor is insignificant, but its contents are extraordinary and of the greatest prophetic importance. It was a command that bridges be constructed across the bay of San Francisco. The project at that time was looked upon as wildly visionary and entirely impracticable. It was received with no credulity and subjected to scornful derision. But a slight survey of the events of that time may disclose some pertinent facts. The overland railroad had just been completed on May 10, 1869, which was a far-reaching event. Stanford and his associates were already attempting to secure Yerba Buena to make it a great terminal depot. Norton's shrewdness and unusual business abilities had suffered no impairment, crazed as he was otherwise. And no man in San Francisco was better qualified to realize the enormous commercial and economic value of those shadowy bridges. Sixty-seven years have elapsed since that proclamation was issued, but the vision of the gentle old Emperor was not so fantastic after all.

In personal appearance the Emperor was always a picturesque and striking figure. He was of medium height, heavy-set, with brown hair that was inclined to curl, heavy eye-brows under a massive forehead, moustache and beard that became a royal personage, and clear and penetrating eyes. His garb was of navy blue cut in military style and profusely adorned with brass buttons. The shoulders were surmounted with massive gilt epaulettes, sometimes tarnished from exposure. In the earlier years of his reign he had worn a military cap embellished with red trimmings, which is quite familiar in the cartoons of the time. About 1865, one of his loyal subjects presented the Emperor with a tall beaver hat, which was thoughtfully decorated with a cockade of feathers and a rosette. The cap had outlived its usefulness and was laid aside forever. The hat, replaced from time to time, continued to be the royal headgear until the close of the Emperor's reign. In 1867, one of his subjects had sent from Oregon a large and unusual specimen of grapevine intended for a walking-stick. It was shod with a ferule and gold-mounted, and thereafter constituted his sceptre. He was never without it, but in inclement weather he carried also an umbrella, knowing wisely that royalty may be drenched and that his Kingly authority was no greater than that of his illustrious predecessor, Canute.

He bore a sort of resemblance to Napoleon III, which fact when commented upon brought forth the ridiculous rumor that Norton was the son of that ill-starred monarch. This misstatement, so obvious in its utter absurdity, was hatched in the scattered brains of some irresponsible contemporary whose living prototypes, loud with vacant volubilities and rich in historical misapplications, are yet in our midst.

The private life of the Emperor was simple. For seventeen years he had lived at the Eureka Lodging House, and the regal apartment was not palatial. It was a room of 6 x 10 feet in dimensions, with threadbare carpet and dis-

STEAMER DAY IN SAN FRANCISCO

abled furniture. The chief mural decorations were portraits of the foreign rulers and his collection of hats. His familiar form was seen and known everywhere. He was a constant attendant of churches, theatres, musical affairs, civic gatherings and school commencements. He was deeply interested in higher education and in the earlier days of the University was a frequent visitor. He was fond of children and to them he was always gentle and courteous. There was at that time a Lyceum of Free Culture of which he was a member, and there he sustained many debates most intelligently and logically. It is said that he had some interest in spiritualism, but in which direction is not known. For sustenance he had the freedom of nearly every restaurant in the city, as also of every saloon. He was unusually abstemious, and if he frequently appeared in the popular saloons of Barry and Patten and "Frank's," or in the famous "Bank Exchange" and the "Pantheon," it was not in quest of liquor, but of "free lunch."

It was his custom to visit the markets and the docks, and to view buildings in progress of construction. This was not from idle curiosity but from genuine interest, for in all these and kindred matters he was keenly informed. From time to time visits were made to men of affairs, but the Emperor had that rare discretion that never permitted himself to be regarded as a nuisance. He was even welcomed, for his own business training had taught him to appear at a suitable time and to retire at a proper moment. He had never met with royalty but once, and the distinguished personage was Dom Pedro, Emperor of Brazil.

No sketch of Norton would be entirely complete without some reference to "Bummer" and "Lazarus," the two dogs that enjoyed the freedom of San Francisco in the sixties. Lazarus was a wretched beast of low degree, and Bummer was but little better. But in some of his long gone ancestors there must have been a strain of nobility, for it was Bummer who sniffed this in the Emperor, and thereafter associated himself with the royal presence, with the miserable Lazarus as humble retainer. This was not of Norton's choice, but—noblesse oblige.

Edward Jump, then a young man, was the popular cartoonist of the sixties. In numerous of his cartoons he had introduced the well-known Emperor. In one of these, Norton is depicted at a free-lunch table, satisfying the royal appetite, and beneath are the two dogs awaiting the crumbs. Bummer as usual is alert and confident; Lazarus stands meanly, looking even more dejected than he did upon the morn of his resurrection. This caricature was displayed in a local shop-window where it was seen by Norton. It was the only time throughout his long reign that he was known to exhibit signs of violence. He savagely growled, "It is an insult to the dignity of an Emperor!" and crashing his stick through the window destroyed the offending print.

Only once was he arrested. In 1867, a newly-appointed, young and zealous deputy apprehended Norton and took him before the Commissioner of Lunacy. The next day when brought before the proper authorities he was promptly discharged with an apology. The verdict was, "that he had shed no blood, robbed no one, and despoiled no country; which is more than can be said of his fellows in that line." There were returned to him the key of the

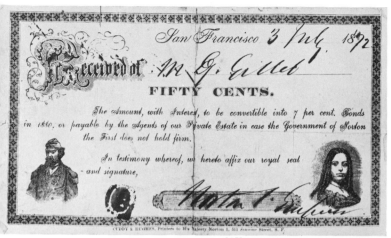

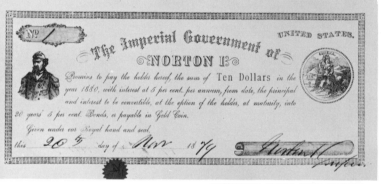

San Francisco 3 July 1872

Received of Mr. G. Gillet

FIFTY CENTS.

The Amount, with Interest, to be convertible into 7 per cent. Bonds in 1880, or payable by the Agents of our Private Estate in case the Government of Norton the First does not hold firm.

In testimony whereof, we hereto affix our royal seal and signature,

CUDDY & HUGHES, Printers to H's Majesty Norton 1, 511 Sansome Street, S. F.

COURTESY: WELLS FARGO BANK

No. 1

The Imperial Government of NORTON I

UNITED STATES.

Promises to pay the holder hereof, the sum of Ten Dollars in the year 1880, with interest at 5 per cent. per annum, from date, the principal and interest to be convertible, at the option of the holder, at maturity, into 20 years 5 per cent. Bonds, or payable in Gold Coin.

Given under our Royal hand and seal.

this 20th day of Nov 1879

COURTESY: CALIF. HIST. SOCIETY

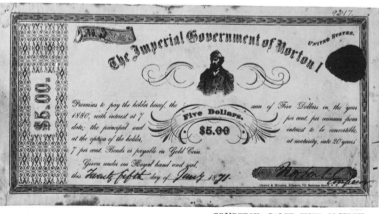

The Imperial Government of Norton I

UNITED STATES.

$5.00

Promises to pay the holder hereof, the sum of Five Dollars in the year 1880, with interest at 7 per cent. per annum from date; the principal and interest to be convertible, at the option of the holder, at maturity, into 20 years 7 per cent. Bonds or payable in Gold Coin.

Five Dollars. $5.00

Given under our Royal hand and seal, this Twenty fifth day of June 1871.

Cuddy & Hughes, Printers, 511 Sansome Street, S. F.

COURTESY: CALIF. HIST. SOCIETY

EXAMPLES OF NORTON'S IMPERIAL SCRIPT

palace, and the imperial funds amounting to $4.75 lawful money. For these the Emperor gave his royal receipt.

During all these years the Emperor had lived. From June 15, 1858, he had been a charter member of Occidental Lodge, F. and A. M., and the Masons, it is said, had paid his room rent. Voluntary subscriptions were made by the faithful among his subjects, and when the treasury was depleted he was accustomed to levy a tax of varying but small amounts. For these he invariably gave or offered a receipt in the form of a promissory note. This was a printed scrip which bore a vignette of the Emperor and was payable in 1880. It had been his purpose to exchange these for a new series, payable in 1890 at 4 per cent.

The last hoax played upon him was also the crowning effort of the graceless, witty scamps of his realm. Norton was induced to believe that by marriage with Queen Victoria, he could bind closer the ties of the two great nations. Telegrams of congratulations upon the approaching happy event were found among his effects. These purported to be from Alexander of Russia, Beaconsfield, Grévy, former President Grant, and others.

The close of the Emperor's life and the end of his long reign came on January 8, 1880. Early in the evening while standing at the corner of California street and Grant avenue, he was observed to fall. Assistance was rendered immediately, but ten minutes later the Emperor was gone. Death had been caused by sanguineous apoplexy. An autopsy by Doctors Stivers and Douglass, made with special reference to the brain, disclosed the fact that the organ was quite normal, and the more unusual fact that it weighed 51 ounces. The costs of the funeral were provided

[53]

by Joseph G. Eastland, R. E. Brewster, and the members of the Pacific Club. The final ceremonies were conducted at the Morgue, and the eulogy was delivered by Rev. N. L. Githens, Rector of the Church of the Advent. It is estimated that 10,000 people of all walks in life came to view that silent figure, which rested in a wilderness of flowers. A lady, well-known and of high social standing, with her own fingers pinned upon the lapel of the sleeping monarch a beautiful boutonniere of hyacinth and a spray of fern, remarking quietly that Norton had been kind to her when she was a child and he was in the heyday of his success. He was interred in Masonic Cemetery.

The old cemetery was closed to interments in 1902. The litigation which followed lasted nearly three decades, but finally the court ordered the property to be abandoned. It was completely dismantled and plowed over.

On June 30, 1934, a beautiful and impressive ceremony took place in Woodlawn cemetery. The occasion was to perpetuate the name of the Emperor, and the event was the unveiling of a stone commemorating him and his peaceful reign. It was made possible once more by the members of the Pacific-Union club, associated with the California Historical Society, the Society of California Pioneers and other kindred organizations. None of the principal members of that earlier ceremony is now surviving, but the legacy of generosity and sympathetic understanding has richly endowed their successors.

For twenty-three years the Emperor had reigned in his fantastic realm. His were the best-known features in San Francisco, and there still live many of the older citizens who yet vividly remember them. A striking portrait of

NORTON I
EMPEROR
OF THE UNITED STATES
AND
PROTECTOR OF MEXICO
—
JOSHUA A. NORTON
1819 — 1880

COURTESY: WELLS FARGO BANK

him, painted by Benoni Irwin, was formerly in the chess-room of the Bohemian club, and a familiar little terra-cotta figure, possibly by Mezzara or Wells, may yet occasionally be seen.

The question of the insanity of Norton has been debated, but the evidence would appear to be in favor of the entire sincerity of his belief. At the time of his disaster he was but thirty-five years of age, and with his great abilities might easily have regained his fortune, or created a new one. But that single, twisted convolution lay uppermost and for twenty-three years dominated his purpose. Poor, sometimes soiled and shabby, pathetic and philosophic, but always with a noble mind, he bore himself with dignity amid his squalid surroundings with one fixed and unvarying purpose, and that was consistently the welfare of his people. The heritage of honor and integrity that he had handed down while in his affluence, was never squandered nor dissipated, and so he bore the respect and goodwill of the best of his people to the end. The jokes played upon him had been harmless, and the merriment that he sometimes excited had been without the bitter venom of ridicule.

If sincere, his was a career of long heroic sacrifice; if an imposter, he must be ranked as one of the most extraordinary of that class who has yet lived. He left no successor. The emoluments of an unattractive throne and an empty royalty were not alluring; there was none strong enough to follow him; and finally the world was entering upon an epoch of materialism in which there is no provision for such a monarch. From that strange stage through the doors of oblivion thus passes forever Norton I, Emperor of the United States, and Protector of Mexico, L'Empereur est mort.

In the same month, at a Low Jinks of the Bohemian club, a gifted and beloved member, the late Dr. George Chismore, presented this beautiful tribute:

NORTON IMPERATOR

"No more through the crowded streets he goes,
   With his shambling gait and shabby clothes,
   And his furtive glance and whiskered nose—
     Immersed in cares of state.

The serpent twisted upon his staff
Is not less carless of idle chaff,
The mocking speech or the scornful laugh,
     Than he who bore it late.

His nerveless hand has released the helm,
But ere the Lethean flood shall whelm
The last faint trace of his fancied realm,
     Let us contrast his fate

With other rulers and other reigns,
Of royal birth or scheming brains,
And see if his crazy life contains
     So much to deprecate.

No traitorous friends, or vigilant foes,
Rippled the stream of his calm repose,
No fear of exile before him 'rose,
     Whose empire was his pate.

No soldiers died to uphold his fame;
He found no pleasure in woman's shame;
For wasted wealth no well-earned blame
     Turned subjects love to hate.

No long and weary struggle with pain;
One sudden throe in his clouded brain
Closed forever his bloodless reign,
    With every man his friend.

For Death alone did he abdicate,
What Emperor, Prince or potentate,
Can long avoid a similar fate
    Or win a better end!"

    The play comes to its end. The shadowy troupers, briefly evoked for review, pass noiselessly over the boards. Some are friendly and amiable; none are terrifying. With all its harmless fads and foibles; its singular fancies and frailties, that ghostly company has had its brief hour upon the stage. The lights grow dim. The curtain slowly descends, and again the forgotten characters of old San Francisco pass into oblivion.

EMPEROR NORTON WITH BUMMER & LAZARUS

BUMMER AND
LAZARUS

BY ANNE BANCROFT

Of San Francisco's citizens in the war-torn early 'sixties there were many who are known today because they filled their niches with distinction. There were generals, railroad builders, merchants, financiers, writers, and eccentrics. In a class by themselves were Bummer and Lazarus. Though they were "only dogs," Bummer and Lazarus, canine citizens of the young city, showed a devotion to each other, and to their self-imposed civic duties, which won for them the love of their contemporaries, and the respect and admiration of all who read of them today.

Much has been written of Bummer and Lazarus, but never has an accurate biography appeared. During their short span of public life they received more personal notices in the daily press than most of their human fellow-citizens, and their obituaries ranked among the most important of the day. Undoubtedly there is much material to be found in diaries and reminiscences of those years. Until the time when these shall have been uncovered the following brief sketch, pieced together from their journalistic notices, and dedicated to their memory, must suffice.

Early in 1860—some say four or five years before—there appeared on the streets of San Francisco a new stray dog. "Bull in his fighting quarters and Newfoundland in his vital parts" he was described. "Pure white and pure black, spotted." He picked up a living by visiting restaurants and free lunch tables, and because of this practice soon became generally known as "Bummer." He chose the east side of Montgomery Street as his special territory, and worked the establishments between Washington and Sacramento with clock-like regularity. Wrote the San Francisco *Bulletin:*

Of the early history of BUMMER, as of many other famous characters that have figured in the world's history, little is known. He is said to have been born on the western prairies, and in the days of his puppyhood he no doubt sported upon the green grass, and wagged his tail in happy innocence and mingled his infantile bark with the laughter of his master's children. He made the journey to California across the plains, fought with the Indians, lost his master, became demoralized, and arrived in Sacramento a disappointed and disgusted dog. The disgust was not lessened by a residence in that one-horse town, and after a brief sojourn there he made his way to San Francisco. . . .

His first journalistic notice appeared in the columns of the *Alta California*, on January 18, 1861, and chronicles the beginning of the friendship that was to bring him undying fame:

. . . Three or four days ago, a poor, lean, mangy cur was attacked in the street by a larger dog, and was getting unmercifully walloped, when BUMMER's ire being aroused at the unequal contest, he rushed in and gave the attacking canine such a rough handling that he was glad to quit the field yelping, and making the best dog time on record. The poor cur had one of his legs half bitten through, and having limped upon the sidewalk, he proceeded to scrape an acquaintance with his deliverer, BUMMER, who thenceforth took him under his special protection. Every night since that, the 'twa dogs' have slept coiled up together close to some doorway—BUMMER always giving the lame cur the inside berth, and trying to keep him as warm as possible. All day, yesterday, as BUMMER walked deliberately up and down his beat, looking into people's faces to see if he could recognize an acquaintance or a lunch-eater, the cur limped to and fro with him, evidently placing the highest confidence in his companion's proceedings, and counting him as his friend and protector. BUMMER seemed to feel the weight of the responsibility, and regarded his sorry-looking protege with pity, not unmingled by contempt at his woe-begone appearance. The two were seen huddled up together in the most fraternal manner, last night after 12 o'clock.

Lazarus, for the woe-begone cur was none other, was usually referred to as an insignificant dog. Yellowish-black in color, he seemed to be "a cross between a cur and a hound, with a dash of the terrier that was not developed until he went into partnership." He was older than Bummer: "some say he was very near, if not quite, the pioneer dog of the town."

After Bummer's heroic rescue of the forlorn Lazarus the dogs were seldom seen or mentioned apart. Between them developed a faith and affection generally lavished by a fond master and his dog one upon the other. For perhaps the first time the two realized the joys of companionable interdependence.

Dogs generally are selfish—every one for himself. But Bummer and Lazarus shared their bones and flesh. In their social relations they shamed mankind and made the authors of our Divorce law blush as they passed. In repose, Bummer lay on the pavement asleep but showing his teeth notwithstanding; Lazarus lay half a length behind him, his head pillowed on Bummer's side fearless of mishaps, clearly confident that no harm could visit him while Bummer was his friend. In a fight Bummer always took the lead, while Lazarus lay back and encouraged him. Bummer did the biting, Lazarus the barking. Bummer's forte was in his teeth, Lazarus's forte was in his tail which wagged fearfully when his friend was in the thick of an encounter. In case of a reverse, which though rare, has happened before now Lazarus discovered a little the most genius. He was smart on a retreat, while Bummer never seemed to know that he was beaten, but kept on showing his teeth till the victor was out of sight.

Their treatment of other dogs was not perhaps what it should be. Bummer was quite too contemptuous—not even saluting one twice his size with any grace, while Lazarus would have fraternized with every mongrel in town if Bummer's head were turned. Like other best of friends their natural dispositions differed. Lazarus preferred early morning walks—it was safer; Bummer was around evenings—it paid best.

Of the two Bummer received far more admiration and respect from his fellow citizens. Lazarus never displayed the complete unselfishness of his canine friend. Commented the *Bulletin:*

Close observers say, that when there was a fat bone which he could snatch unobserved, he was ingenious about getting it in possession. On such occasions he seemed suddenly fond of soli-

A GATHERING OF THE CHARACTERS

tude, and when half an hour later he returned, fetching the bone to share it with his partner, there was not any marrow in the place where the marrow ought to be. Bummer magnanimously pretended never to see these evidences of his friend's bad faith.

An example of ingratitude on the part of Lazarus was chronicled by the *Alta* of April 12, 1861:

Last week some evil-minded person had the cruelty to shoot Bummer, wounding his leg in such a manner that he could scarcely walk. The animal began to mope and slink about in obscure corners, as sick dogs generally do, upon which Lazarus forgetting the generosity of his benefactor, coolly deserted him, trotting off to hunt up more profitable acquaintances, and Bummer experiences the sting of ingratitude. That is, he may be supposed to experience it, for there is no question as to the chivalrous care which he took of his companion when their conditions were reversed. He might console himself, however, with the reflection that such instances are not confined to the canine race.

Bummer and Lazarus were not of the breed that expect something for nothing. They received their sustenance from the hands of the citizens of San Francisco, and in payment assumed the role of City Rat Exterminators. The San Francisco *Bulletin* of October 3, 1863 announced:

The town rings today with stories of their prowess in this line. Gould & Martin last April cleared off a gallery in their fruit market, and during the process the two dogs, with the aid of some clubs wielded by earnest men, killed over 400 rats! That is vouched for as a true story. At another place of business—not a restaurant—when an effort was on foot to get rid of the rats, Bummer and Lazarus killed eighty-five of the vermin in about 20 minutes. . . .

[67]

We learn something of the methods of these rat-killers extraordinaire from the following:

In front of the Clay Street French market we have seen two or three men for a day's sport tear up the sidewalk and begin to shovel out live rats, two to the spade, not one of them could strike the ground without meeting Bummer's fierce teeth half way. Then it was fearful to see Lazarus shake the poor broken-backed creatures. Occasionally, Bummer would fall back and wait for Lazarus to go in, and then it was delightful to see how his bushy tail was affected with joy of his weak friend's enterprise. Between the two, no rat ever saw the light of their eyes and escaped alive. . . . Nothing could stand before them . . . and they shared alike the profits of their enterprise. . . .

While Bummer and Lazarus worked hard at their self-appointed task, they refused to submit to any that were imposed upon them. A rural visitor once asked a reporter where he could get a good shepherd dog. The reporter, seeing a chance to get a good home for Bummer, recommended him and saw him taken off to Alameda's hills. Bummer was put in charge of a flock of sheep. The experiment was disastrous to several fancy rams. As the *Bulletin* put it:

Bummer doubtless fancied them a higher style of rats, and treated them accordingly. In his proper line of freeing the city of rats he was unapproachable; but as you would not set Gilmore's Swamp Angel to belching Greek fire to illuminate a peaceful city, so it was impossible even to put Bummer in the wrong place.

One Saturday night, by some chance, Bummer was locked in a news depot. Lazarus, disconsolate, searched for his friend.

Lazarus traveled Montgomery street, visited all his old haunts, hunted high and low, refused food, was inconsolable all Sunday. On Monday morning he did not even go to Chase's for breakfast, but resumed his search. Passing the shop where Bummer lay solitary among the literature, he heard a scratching on the window. Instantly Lazarus made a dive at the window, for it was his long lost brother. The plate glass was shivered to atoms, the friends were united, and together they strolled when the doors were opened, into the light of day. On another occasion, a party, either heedless, or thinking he would make rats thinner on his premises thereby, locked them both together in a jeweller's shop. There was a terrible scene in that party's premises next morning—valuables scattered, invaluables ruined! Nobody made the mistake of locking them inside again! They were the best friends of the community when independent and at liberty— worse than iconoclasts, when caged.

And what a contrast is the following picture! Quoth the *Alta* of June 14, 1862:

Yesterday we observed the four-legged Damon and Pythias stretched out together on the sidewalk, away up Washington street, and snoozing cosily under the hot rays of the noonday sun.

Bummer and Lazarus were not the only stray dogs in San Francisco. There were others less useful, less loved and petted. They became so numerous that it became expedient to establish a city pound, and to incarcerate all unlicensed or uncared for animals. But the dog-slayer was unfamiliar with the peculiarities of the citizens who employed him. He assumed that his instructions referred to ALL unlicensed dogs. He captured Lazarus.

Great was the excitement resulting! Consternation ruled. It had been assumed that Bummer and Lazarus were above the rank of mere unknown and unwanted canines. It seemed for a time that the end had come to the faithful friendship. Public sentiment was aroused to the point of action. One citizen, said to have been F. Martin, Esq., went to the pound, claimed ownership, and bailed Lazarus out of his prison. The matter did not rest here, however. Public sentiment had been raised to greater heights. Sponsored by this same benefactor, a demand was laid before the city fathers, and a special ordinance was passed granting to Bummer and Lazarus the freedom of the city.

The *Alta* of June 17, 1862, commented on the "unparalleled sagacity" of the two dogs on this occasion:

Whether the dogs Bummer and Lazarus were aware or not of the fact that a memorial was to be presented for their release last evening, certain it is that at the hour of convening the Board of Supervisors they lay crouched at the threshhold of the chamber, apparently eager to hear what was to be said and done for their benefit. If any man carried them there, it was a cute dodge to get favorable action on their petition; if they went there voluntarily, they ought to have free run of the town during the rest of their lives!

A week later they substantially proved their worth as well as their appreciation. A runaway team was seen dashing up Clay street. On one side, in hot pursuit, ran Bummer, on the other Lazarus.

On reaching the corner of Kearny, BUMMER rushed in front of the horse and held him at bay until a man came up and caught the team, LAZARUS being on hand to check any further advance.

A gesture of gratitude from the city's chief ratters.

TOMPSON IN A QUANDARY.
SAN FRANCISCO "LOCAL HITS" CROSS READINGS TO BE READ DOWNWARDS.
APPLETON GEN'L AGENT 508 MONTGOMERY ST SAN FRANCISCO.

BUMMER, LAZARUS AND OTHER CHARACTERS

But it was not long before they were again the subject of a notorious episode. The *Alta* of July 13 tells the story:

The canine paupers, Bummer and Lazarus, having been granted the freedom of the town by our City Fathers, the latter of course are responsible for their good behavior, and liable for their misdeeds. Lazarus got locked in Rosenfield's Stationery Store, on Montgomery Street yesterday, having hid himself to get a good 'snooze.' Towards night he awoke to find himself in secure quarters. He tried to break jail, but it was no go. He dashed his head against the thick plate glass, cracking it in several places, then jumped on the cases and smashed up various delicate and valuable articles with perfect recklessness. Bummer came along, but could give him no aid, and at midnight Lazarus occupied the show window bench, whilst his brother kept watch outside. The town may have a nice little bill of damages to pay for these canine pranks!

Bummer and Lazarus appear in many of the cartoons of San Francisco in the 'sixties, particularly in those of Edward E. Jump. One of these gave rise to the erroneous assertion that the two dogs belonged to Emperor Norton, who was also included upon every occasion. In the well known cartoon the three are seen at a free lunch table. Emperor Norton, golden epaulets and plumed hat gracing his imperial uniform, is seen spearing a tasty morsel into his mouth. Beside him, and looking up at him with sniffing wistfulness, are Bummer and Lazarus. The cartoon was displayed in one of the downtown store windows, where it was seen by His Imperial Majesty. Angered at the pictorial reference to his financial condition, and the presentation of himself to his subjects in such an undignified occupation, the Emperor raised his cane and smashed the plate glass window.

From January, 1861, to November, 1862, the canine friendship continued and grew to be one of the features of San Francisco. Then tragedy struck. The San Francisco *Bulletin* of October 3, 1862 announced:

Lazarus is dead. He began to swell up in the course of the night, and passed gently away before the hour that Bummer has generally given him a rat for his morning meal. . . .

It was Bummer that always showed his teeth, but Lazarus was charged yesterday with having bitten a boy, and it is thought that the boy's father threw the poison that made Lazarus grow in a night too fat to live! The dog that had no enemy dies by violence, while he who was the terror of all the rats on the coast survives! The party that claimed to own Lazarus, because he bailed him out of the Pound once and got the Supervisors to ease his case over with a special ordinance, has offered a reward of $50 for the discovery of the man who threw the poison. The brevity of this article is due to our consideration that the people read the newspapers and believe them, and we do not want to so prejudice the community that when the slayer of Lazarus is indicted it will be impossible to get a jury.

The city mourned. Edward E. Jump has left us a fanciful portrayal of the funeral of Lazarus. A grave is being dug for the departed dog, who is held aloft on a stretcher. Emperor Norton, in flowing robes, is reading the burial service. The line of mourners, among whom may be seen many of Lazarus's human friends, winds across the back of the picture. At the end is the dog-slayer, with his wagon which bears a huge cage out of which protrude an enormous number of tails. Around the wheels of this equipage are several canine mourners. Directly behind the body of Lazarus walks Bummer, poor old Bummer who now must walk alone.

FUNERAL OF LAZARUS

A long obituary, "A Lament for Lazarus," appeared in the San Francisco *Bulletin*. A large part of it I have already quoted.

. . . These two were very famous dogs. . . . Either alone might never have been worthy of an item—together, they were an institution like the Consolidation Act, or the Emperor Norton, whom everybody knew. Their portraits are in the windows. Their *cartes de visites* are in all well regulated albums. . . .

Other dogs live to eat, and fawn upon their masters; Bummer and Lazarus lived to exterminate rats. Lazarus had no master but Bummer; while poor Bummer was an orphan and never had a master. . . . Bummer was an honest dog—Lazarus a faithful one. . . .

The taxidermists are busy stuffing Lazarus's skin today, and the newspaper men are busy writing their finest eulogies. In our feeble attempt we have perhaps glorified the living Bummer more than the departed Lazarus, gliding unwillingly into that course because we cannot help thinking a living Bummer is better than a dead dog. Besides, the better part of Lazarus still lives —in his friend, without whom he would have been unworthy of an epitaph, his memory survives. Bummer is still around, and the rats lie low.

By the end of the month the result of the efforts of the taxidermists was commended by the *Alta:*

So natural does the canine appear, that BUMMER, the surviving companion of the deceased, gave positive evidence by his manner that he believed LAZARUS had been only sleeping.

The *Bulletin* was so impressed with the seeming immortality thus trust upon Lazarus that it burst into almost half a column of description, praise, and even poetry.

Lazarus has risen, and is stuffed. A skillful taxidermist has taken away from him all that was fleshy, and left of him only what is imperishable. Bright dogs can never die! Lazarus sits in state, looking more natural than he did in life. His appointments are better. Formerly he had to lie on the pavement, now he reposes on a piece of velvet carpeting. Poets are served in the same way. They live in garrets till they die, and then they are put into Westminster Abbey. The world that refused them meat gives them a monument—alive they asked for bread, dead and their countrymen give them a stone. In his new condition Lazarus looks bright and erect—there is a vigilant expression in his eye, as though he smelt a rat. At the same time an expression lingers on his countenance, as though he had done something wrong in dying and getting stuffed before Bummer. It is the first time he ever took precedence of his companion, and probably will be the last. Poor Lazarus, he is mortified that he was not permitted to share his stuffing with Bummer, who always divided his bones with him. Nor is there room for Bummer on the carpet. He has visions of his old friend and companion stretched out on stones while he himself is on velvet. Lovely in their lives, in their death the friends had to be divided. A jeremiad might be written, but where shall be look for a Tupper to gracefully perform the grateful duty. How the author of Proverbial Philosophy and other verbiage would have expanded with the theme. Given, two dogs with but a single bark, two tails that wagged as one, a death and a separation, and what might not a Tupper have done. The "Greeting to Alexandria" would have been nowhere beside the Farewell to Lazarus. Would not his numbers have run something thus?

> 100,000 Pities,
> 100,000 Pities,
> And 100,000 more!
> O shining skin of Lazarus,
> Stuffed out to put upon the Plaza as
> No dog was stuffed before.
> Sleep on—let Bummer snore,
> And chase for rats the city o'er,
> But you'll not do it any more.

> 100,000 Pities,
>   And 100,000 more.
> Let all the canines roar
> The dog-gone city o'er,
> And let the steeples chime it—
>   100,000 Pities,
>   And 100,000 more.
> And let the Tupper rhyme it—
> Though Tupper is a bore—
> And sing from door to door!
>   100,000 Pities,
>   And 100,000 more!

If the above is not what Martin Farquhar would have written, it is certainly very near it. And the honors and title which the Prince of Wales conferred on him for the Alexandrine verses would be as nothing to the decorations and emoluments which our Emperor would have showered on him—the freedom of the city and access to all the free lunches about town, given under the Imperial hand and seal.

Lazarus in his present state was introduced to Bummer. Bummer evidently recognized him as his long lost brother, and commenced a search for the strawberry mark, but that had gone to seed. Bummer seemed to know that a wondrous change had come over his friend, and was puzzled to account for it. Not as of old did he arise and offer Bummer the softest plank to lie down upon, happy and content if he could only rest his head on Bummer's flank. Bummer saw there was a mystery and looked awestruck. He may not have known that Lazarus was behind the curtain and familiar with problems that were blinding to him; he may not have known that whether rats were large or small, scarce or plenty, was all one to Lazarus now. But he certainly looked and acted as though he were impressed, and wandered away with a softer expression about his grim nether jaw than it has known for many long years.

The name of the taxidermist who has given Lazarus to immortality is E. F. Lorquin. The task is well done, and at a cost of about $50. F. Martin, whom Lazarus was wont to follow before breakfast and obey before dinner in life, has been the prime mover in the matter and footer of the bill. But for the body of Lazarus there are many claimants. The Pioneers want it, and the Supervisors are likely to make overtures. But these latter would probably serve the dog as they served the aerolite a few years ago. To no one individual or association should the honor of keeping the remains be entrusted—pass them around.

Little is known of Bummer's activities during the next three years. Once in an article dealing with the terribly dusty condition of San Francisco's streets we catch a glimpse of the lonely dog.

Fitz Smythe insists that on Saturday he saw old Bummer lying in Merchant Street, and that on the moment that he dropped his under jaw in a yawn and straightened out his hind leg, about six inches, the dust which arose from the movement entirely obscured him from view, and caused people to run into their houses and close the doors, under the impression that a compound of the simoon and whirlwind was coming down the street.

Once, briefly, was his solitude broken. In the *Alta* of January 12, 1864, we read of an attempt to form a new partnership:

Bummer having worn the weeds of mourning for the usual period, and having arrived at the time when Fashion permits her votaries to become genteelly consolable, and commence looking around for a new comforter, has given the memory of his late lamented friend and fellow-traveller the shake; he has formed a new partnership, and is now going from place to place holding ratification meetings in honor of the event. The new partner in

[80]

the firm—Lazarus, Jr.—is a likely looking bull pup, not yet arrived to full size and age of usefulness, but bids fair to eventually rival his great namesake and predecessor in activity and affection for the senior partner in the concern.

What ended the friendship no one knows, but there is no further mention of Lazarus Jr.

Poor Bummer was once again to be the object of wanton cruelty. On September 14, 1865, the *Alta* announced:

Some weeks since a drunken bummer, who ought at least to roast in a place as hot as the Upper Sacramento Valley for the term of his natural life, or longer, kicked poor old Bummer down a stairway on Montgomery Street and injured him so that he has never recovered and is not likely to ever recover. His body is now swollen to twice its usual size, and the poor old fellow appears to be at death's door.

The wrath of the city was roused against the drunken Henry Rippey. He was arrested "for kicking old Bummer as he lay asleep in the sun; also for kicking the amazed old pensioner down a stairs. He was fiercely rebuked by the Court and fined $100 and costs." Lacking funds Rippey went to jail. His cell-mate, David Popley, "a popcorn seller, who was arrested for popping a man on the smeller," shared the general feeling of anger and disgust, and punctuated it with a well-aimed blow at Rippey.

Bummer died on the morning on November 2, 1865. A chronicle of his last days appeared in the *Bulletin:*

EXIT 'BUMMER'—The old canine celebrity of San Francisco, surnamed BUMMER, long petted and beloved by her citizens, is dead. It is generally known that he had been on the decline for some weeks past, and many a lesson in *memento mori* has he taught to his fellow bummers who gathered around his prostrate form as he lay on the sidewalk on Clay street, gasping for breath and apparently in the last agonies. These deceptive appearances had been so often followed by a sudden revival of animation and apparent health in the poor dog that many came to regard them as theatrical tricks ignobly resorted to by old BUMMER in his second childhood, to test the public sympathy and see whether he had not outlived his popularity as well as his usefulness. But those who did him the grievous injustice of such an insinuation will now see their error. BUMMER was not a dog to resort to tricks at any period of his life, for any purpose. He died as he lived, open and above board, BUMMER by name, bummer by nature, no more or less. It was evident to those who saw him on the sidewalk yesterday afternoon that the period of his dissolution was fast approaching and so it proved. As the shades of evening gathered around his eyelids and 'night drew her sable curtain down and pinned it with a star', (the dog star), BUMMER grew rapidly worse, and at three o'clock this morning yielded up the ghost without a murmur or a bark. . . .

To many of his old friends this was a hard blow, and the news was difficult to accept. The *Alta* flatly denied it.

Old Bummer still lives in spite of the murderous obituary notices written by those who have long disputed with him for precedence at the free lunch tables, and would be but too happy to count him out of the ring. He is worth a dozen of his would-be mourners yet.

Two days later even the *Alta* was forced to admit that it had been scooped, and that Bummer had indeed left this earth.

BUMMER IS DEAD!—The ancient Bummer's death was posted on the canine *Bulletin* board some days since, but we hesitated to

EARTH *QUAKEY* TIMES,
SAN FRANCISCO, OCT. 8, 1865.

BUMMER IN EARTH QUAKEY TIMES

accept the mournful tidings as correct on such doubtful authority. Later and more reliable information confirms the report,
however, and we tearfully give place to the following:

ELEGY ON BUMMER

by

A. Bohemian, Esq.

He, who was faithful to the end,
　　The noble Bummer sleeps;
Gone hence to join his better friend,
　　Where doggy never weeps.

All tears are wiped from Bummer's eyes,
　　Good angels give him place;
E'en at the Gates of Paradise,
　　Barking glad notes of grace.

When Lazarus was ill, in need,
　　'Twas Bummer bro't him bread;
Then brethren all, I pray take heed,
　　To gain such praise when dead.

Ben Adhem's angel, in his log,
　　Writes first to love their fellow-men;
Be careful he don't place a dog
　　Where he should place you, with his pen.

News of Bummer's demise spread to the state of Nevada,
and no less a person than Samuel Clemens wrote his obituary in the *Territorial Enterprise.* I quote it as reprinted
in the *Californian* of November 11:

EXIT BUMMER—As we have devoted but little space to an event
which has filled our local contemporaries with as much sorrow
(judging from the columns of lamentation it has called forth) as
would the decease of the best biped in the city, we give 'Mark

Twain's' view of the occurrence, as recorded in the *Enterprise* of the 8th. Strangely enough, Mark, who can't stand 'ballad inflection' seems to think there has not been quite enough of 'Bummer':

"The old vagrant BUMMER is really dead at last; and although he was always more respected than his obsequious vassal, the dog LAZARUS, his exit has not made half as much stir in the newspaper world as signalized the departure of the latter. I think it is because he died a natural death: died with friends around him to smooth his pillow and wipe the death-damps from his brow, and receive his last words of love and resignation; because he died full of years, and honor, and disease, and fleas. *He* was permitted to die a natural death, as I have said, but poor LAZARUS 'died with his boots on'—which is to say, he lost his life by violence; he gave up the ghost mysteriously, at dead of night, with none to cheer his last moments or soothe his dying pains. So the murdered dog was canonized in the newspapers, his shortcomings excused and his virtues heralded to the world; but his superior, parting with his life in the fullness of time, and in the due course of nature, sinks as quietly as might the mangiest cur among us. Well, let him go. In earlier days he was courted and carressed; but latterly he had lost his comliness—his dignity had given place to want of self respect, which allowed him to practise mean deceptions to regain for a moment that sympathy and notice which had become necessary to his very existence, and it was evident to all that the dog had had his day; his great popularity had gone forever. In fact, Bummer should have died sooner: there was a time when his death would have left a lasting legacy of fame to his name. Now, however, he will be forgotten in a few days."

But Bummer has never been forgotten, and when his death was reported in the *Reese River Reveille*, it was added that his hide, like that of Lazarus, was to be stuffed and displayed in one of the saloons at whose free lunch tables he had so often dined.

As a companion piece to Jump's *Funeral of Lazarus*,

COURTESY: ALBERT DRESSLER

POOR OLD BUMMER

Snooks, Jr., another famous cartoonist of the day, presented *Poor Old Bummer!* Here we see the swollen corpse of Bummer laid on a draped bier, with candles at head and feet. The mass of mourners includes many faces famous in civic, military, and literary life. Emperor Norton, looking somewhat like Alice's Carpenter, has just paid his respects at the bier. Overhead above the clouds are two bat-like canine cherubs, the re-united Souls of Bummer and Lazarus.

Thus, as it must to all men, death came to the noble Bummer.

. . . he has been the pet of everybody, "without distinction of party." He has figured in all the sketches and caricatures of San Francisco life as prominently as other town celebrities, and the announcement of his demise will call up memories and associations in the minds of San Franciscans, now travelling in distant lands, quite as vivid as would be produced by more important events. His remarkable friendship for the insignificant dog LAZA-RUS (since his ascension known as *Alta Lazarus*) will now doubtless meet its reward, and the twain can once more walk side by side, the chief lazzoroni of the canine heaven.

PORTRAIT OF NORTON I BY ADDIE BALLOU

PERSONAL RECOLLECTIONS
OF NORTON I

EMPEROR OF THE UNITED STATES*

BY ADDIE L. BALLOU

Treasured for many years among the archives of relics
and curios, in the Pioneer building, that perished with the
holocaust of April 18, 1906, were a few mementoes of
early days in the history of San Francisco, valued and
sacred principally for their associations, more honored in
their decadence by care of preservation than in their active
service, were the surviving relics of past time characters
peculiar to San Francisco.

Incidentally of the once famous "twa dogs," Bummer
and Lazarus, the stiff and stuffy hides which suggested
no pride of ancestry or pedigree superior to the ordinary

*Reprinted with the permission of the San Francisco *News-Call Bulletin*
from the issue of the San Francisco *Sunday Call*, September 27, 1908.

small cur, they were the city's adopted waifs and endowed with virtues which appealed to the many human waifs of varying degree, with such masterfulness as to immortalize their memories with embalmment under taxidermic skill, duly labeled and set up after demise. Bummer arrived unannounced, probably by some passing vessel, was forsaken and forgotten, and, shirking for himself, soon became familiar with ways of foraging adapted to his need and, being of honest habits, waited with regularity at the market place for his meals, to then disappear with a grateful wag of his abbreviated tail until mess time came again.

Where he took lodging was not definitely known. He soon acquired and responded to the name of Bummer, and was known and respected far and near for vices which he might have acquired but virtuously refrained from.

One morning Bummer appeared with an air of understanding and approval, accompanied by a brother canine in distress. Somewhere he had picked up a forlorn, broken legged dog, evidently as homeless as himself, and bringing him to the market, asked in his dog appealing way that the unfortunate might share his food, waiting beside him and licking his wound meantime. Sympathizing hands bound the broken leg, which soon healed, but the comradeship of the two dogs never ceased while both lived, and they were known as Bummer and Lazarus.

Near by, and conspicuous in their glass case preservative, duly labeled, was the exhibit, the uniform and acouterments wont to habilitate the person of the erstwhile man of destiny, empty now as were the honors claimed by their illustrious wearer, self styled Norton I, emperor of the United States and protector of Mexico. Perhaps, though, best exemplified by the term "pretender" was this one time universally known landmark of old San Francisco, from its primitive days till the time of his death at some 70 years of age, more or less. He arrived in this city on November 5, 1849, via Rio Janeiro and Valparaiso from South Africa, where, it is said, he passed his youth indifferently at the cape of Good Hope, and for some years he occupied himself in business in the ordinary way among businessmen. He became possessor of considerable realty near the present site of the city hall. He invested in ventures of shipping teas and coffees from the tropics, it is stated, and the loss of one of his cargoes was in part responsible for his assumption of the reins of government as emperor of the United States and plenipotentiary extraordinary to Mexico.

Whatever the line of his incarnation might have been will doubtless remain a mystery, confident though he was, through the testimony of a fellow comrade of the king's own Horse Guard, a reliable witness at Buckingham palace, that he was, or by rights should have been, the son of his majesty George IV and Queen Caroline, though possibly he was, or might have been, changed in the cradle at the time of his birth, but that by some unexplained transfer or substitution his rights had been usurped, but when the time came to assert them he should come into his own. California had recognized his authority by declaring him through the legislature of 1852-3 emperor of California, but the act was suppressed because he would not give up the national cause.

With never failing assertiveness he watched the growth and prosperity of the city from hill to hill and to the

Golden gate, and the approach of many well laden ships as they entered, with a paternal pride, and directed the commercial and other interests of the nation with a supervision alike unique and unquestioned.

Familiar to every business house, and child of earlier days a fragment of the history of the city, as was the pathetic yet characteristic ability of everything pertaining to it to care for itself or find recognition of its needs by other kindly people, as did the "twa dogs," was this calm, peaceful arbiter of the city's well being undisturbed of his self-assumed power.

His undisputed territory offered gratis transportation within the city wherever his unmeasured interests took him, though not at all times so successful in attempting longer trips. The writer's first acquaintance with his majesty was on first arriving in the city, when boarding a streetcar from the general postoffice there also entered a heavily epauletted figure otherwise adorned with various devices, badges and ribbons and bearing the inseparable, massive, snakehead sword cane, which as he claimed, was sent him by the king of one of the south sea islands, his ever present faded umbrella and an awesome presence, and seated himself opposite. The conductor passed through the car collecting fares without slighting him. Immediately there was the attitude of affront and offended dignity as he rose to the occasion.

"What do you mean, sir, asking your emperor for money? Don't you know whom you are talking to? I shall have you discharged if you do not attend to your business better hereafter," was the quick but effective retort, much to the amusement of the passengers observing the incident.

There was not in the whole city one more seemingly ever present. There was no church or public meeting of importance that did not find him a frequent listener and sometimes a participant in the deliberations thereof, and his appearance was always striking and picturesque. His motley and variegated dress and equipage; his ill kept suit of army blue with brass buttons, frayed gold lace, and the ponderous and impossible epaulets heavily fringed, the old gray beaver hat adorned with eagle feathers, plucked mayhap from the thanksgiving bird of the barnyard and banquet; the indispensable faded umbrella tucked under his arm; no one could see and forget that once familiar personality, buttonholed and beribboned with the emblems of his royalty, though dimmed and dust eaten with departed years of use, too venerated even his linen for vulgar laundrying. His massive shoulders had not borne the weight of his responsibilities (and epaulets) without effect. Silhouetted against every day's background, this gentleman of majestic, if not convincing and unobtrusive pretensions, bestrode the city and won for himself in the simplicity of his demeanor the consideration of the entire populace, and no one was there to do or wish him ill.

If he entered the flower gardens to replenish his boutonniere at will, or entered a candy store with a child and ordered candy for the little one, it was never refused on credit, as he did with uncertain regularity; or approached the businessmen and levied a more regular tax upon their "exchequers" he seldom went away empty handed; though the proposed tax of thousands might be responded to in a few fractions of a dollar, he accepted the lesser with as becoming a courtesy as if the sum in demand, and as if by rights his own.

While appreciative of kind words, he was not to be slighted or contemptuously treated with impunity, or without resentment, and his authority was not unsparing of reproach. While ruler and monarch of the United States and protector of Mexico his dominion was to be observed over the seas and rivers, always, otherwise his proclamations were issued as evidenced below:

PROCLAMATION

We, Norton I, Dei gratia emperor of the United States and protector of Mexico, having been refused a passage by the steam navigation company to proceed to Sacramento city, do hereby command the revenue cutter Schubrick to blockade the Sacramento river and to bring them to terms.

(Seal)   NORTON I
                              SAN FRANCISCO, 8TH FEB., 1866.

As there was never any announcement of the blockade as per proclamation, it may be presumed that a compromise was arranged or the proclamation nullified and forgotten.

Over the door of an unpretentious tenement in Commercial street between Kearny and Montgomery there used to hang the transparency in euphonious legend against the lamplight "Rooms to let, 25 and 50 cents per night." Up a rickety stairway to the first floor there was a narrow hall or passageway out of which small rooms were entered, one of which served as executive and sleeping chamber for his royalty. Motley accumulations of remote years were here congregated, a veritable museum of the antique.

His room, small and obscure even to dinginess, was quite too limited to serve as the abode of an empress had he chosen to select one, which he confidently informed the writer he had made provision for several years before while at the cape of Good Hope, when he had met and espoused the hand of Queen Victoria, but fate decreed otherwise when Prince Albert, crossing the horizon, "bulldozed" him out of his bride.

His couch lacked much of the regal and consisted of an antique and very much worn frame, rickety springs and badly soiled and shabby upholstering, valuable principally to its owner, who no doubt found as much peace and repose upon its discouraged appearing surface as his weight of avoirdupois and responsibilities would have permitted in more sumptuous halls, and perhaps an equal conduciveness to the extravagance of his dreams of exalted means and powers. His limited wardrobe depended from tenpenny nails driven into the walls, and was varied and sacred through tradition and long usage.

But the emperor failed not in extending to a casual visitor the courtesies due his rank and title with an unperturbed gravity which ever marked him master of every situation which befell him, and which he would graciously rehearse in manifold volume to his interested hearers, and he was a royal host when recounting the marvelous incidents of his eventful life. He confessed to a little jealousy and international strife between France and England over the honor and distinction of his nativity, in particular since his assumption of the reins of government as emperor of the United States and plenipotentiary extraordinary to Mexico. His various edicts and proclamations denoted his desire to rule justly over a just and incorrupt government according to his own undisputed testimony. In 1860 President Buchanan sent a fraternal letter of recognition, saying: "The strength of your power and the wisdom of your government alone can save the rebellious state of South Carolina," while Napoleon III in complimenting the claims and work of Norton I praised him as a conciliator in his proclamation that brought the Alabama and Kearsage amicably together in French waters barring a slight passage at arms in the imperial government of the United States and Mexico in honor of the event when the former country surrendered Mason and Slidell to the latter. It was regrettable that General Grant had not consulted him for assistance while waiting for the surrender of the southern armies in the war of the rebellion.

When his full rights were established he intended to abolish state constitutions and provide a national one instead, to do away with presidential elections and institute offices from the president down, because this would do away with a vast waste of money in tomfoolery, to make up for which it became necessary for Tom, Dick and Harry to steal everything they can lay hands on.

The coin bearing the crest of Norton I, he claimed, was current in Mexico and Japan, while he was proud to exhibit as curios autograph greetings of Queen Victoria, Gambetta and Bismarck, whose governments he at times felt called upon to reprove.

The good will of the ladies was at all times of importance to him and he always courteously tipped his hat to those of his acquaintance, in passing. He readily sat to the writer for the only portrait on canvas he would consent to pose for, and which met his approval, as he said, "even to the shoe brush on the tip of his nose." He was a faithful artist's model, and when the portrait was completed he drew up a check for $250 on the Nevada bank, which was more honored in the preservation of as a relic than in the cashing at the counter of that bank's treasury. During the sittings, for which he came with regularity, he revealed many confidences relative to his wonderful history.

On being approached as to the matter of regret of his subjects in the choice of his single loneliness of life, he admitted the expediency he might have displayed for his provinces, but confessed to a personal diffidence with the fair sex, inasmuch as they all seemed very modestly "shy" of him, but acquiesced to the suggestion that they were naturally embarrassed and awed at any personal attentions from royalty, inasmuch as titles and coronets were not in a strictly normal sense an American product or acquisition, and the matter of a conjunction with anything regal must at once appeal to their sense of delicacy, particularly whereas he failed to show any inclination to pursue his suit. He thereupon concluded that it would be more in keeping with his exalted position to appoint a chamber of deputies, whose duties would require their immediate conference and action in the matter.

The co-operation of the San Francisco press was ever ready to voice the edicts of an emperor who interested himself so humanely, as may be seen in the following:

PROCLAMATION

The "emperor," recognizing the fact that the Star has the

largest ciculation, handed us the following and requested its insertion:

Whereas, a war vessel belonging to our friend the emperor of Japan is on a visit and is at present in our harbor; and whereas, we are desirous of being courteous to strangers; now, therefore, we, Norton I, Dei gratia emperor, do hereby command all persons to show the officers and crew every attention, so that commerce may be benefited thereby.

NORTON I

Given under our royal hand and seal this 23d December, 1875.

Still earlier appeared the following, which indicated his desire to add to the immigration then so desirable to California:

PROCLAMATION

In view of the large number of emigrants coming to this city, and being desirous that they shall be assisted and protected, we, Norton I, emperor, etc., do hereby order that the Mechanics' pavilion building be immediately prepared for their reception and for transacting their business in order that they may not be fleeced through the rapacity of landlords. The state treasurer is also directed to see that the emigrants are provided with sufficient money to proceed to their respective destinations, and charge the same to the emigration fund, and take bonds from said emigrants for the repayment of such moneys when able to do so.

Done at our city of San Francisco this 21st day of April, 1875.

NORTON I

That the general health of the republic was of first importance to his majesty, no further proof need obtain than is set forth in this

PROCLAMATION

Whereas, the ravages of the cholera in the state of Tennessee continue to increase frightfully, and, whereas, we are desirous that the plague shall be obliterated promptly; now, therefore, we, Norton I, Dei gratia emperor of the United States and protector of Mexico, do hereby order and decree that the whole medical fraternity of the United States, for the present, be placed under the control of the authorities of the state; and any doctor ordered from one locality to another, who shall refuse to obey these requests, shall be fined and imprisoned as the gravity of the case may warrant.

NORTON I

A bit of satire as well as caution appears in the forceful and adroit charge which appeared in May, 1876, in this brief but characteristic

PROCLAMATION

Whereas, Sitting Bull and the United States army have had their fun about long enough. Now, therefore, we, Norton I, Dei gratia emperor, do hereby command the immediate return of Crook and Terry to headquarters, and Sitting Bull is commanded with his whole tribe to surrender to the emperor, whose will is that justice is done, as otherwise, sooner or later, the death of himself and tribe is certain.

NORTON I

On the date of the same publication also appears the evidence of his far-reaching protection and good will toward a sister republic, viz:

Whereas, we intend assisting Mexico with funds, and desire also that the United States and Mexico should have the interest reduced by indorsement of the emperor on the national debt. Now, therefore, we, Norton I, command all and every person to desist from committing depredation on his private personal estate and the enemy arrested who persists in injuring the prestige of the emperor by crying fraud and thereby leading people astray.

DEI GRATIA NORTON I

EMPEROR OF UNITED STATES AND PROTECTOR OF MEXICO

That he favored hospitable relations with the Orient has here proof:

PROCLAMATION

The following telegram has been received by His Imperial Majesty Norton I:

Dear Brother—It is with extreme regret that I receive yours announcing the nonarrival of the $14,000,000 which I forwarded you some time since. Be assured that the matter will be immediately looked into, and no stone left unturned looking to the receiving and safe delivery to you of the coin.

HOI TANG, EMPEROR

The emperor commands the persons who are in possession of this money to forthwith give up possession of the coin under penalty of our supreme displeasure.

NORTON I

The destruction of the relics of this strange and kindly old man, who once filled so much space in the old San Francisco, left little to hold him in memory; and he who lives his three score years and leaves no thorn within another's breast has earned an imperishable tablet.

Whatever of mystery in relation to the real tragedy of the lone old man's past may have been locked up within the cabinet of his own consciousness, or was reclothed in the fabric of his peculiar dream life, he was consistent at all times with himself, each act, proclamation or day as each succeeded the other, and his pretensions never belied each other.

A
PORTRAIT GALLERY
OF
EMPEROR NORTON I

COURTESY: CALIF. HIST. SOCIETY

COURTESY: CALIF. HIST. SOCIETY

COURTESY: WELLS FARGO BANK

COURTESY: CALIF. HIST. SOCIETY

COURTESY: WELLS FARGO BANK

COURTESY: CALIF. HIST. SOCIETY

COURTESY: BANCROFT LIBRARY

An Edict.

His Imperial Majesty, Norton I., has issued
the following edict to Hall McAllister, Esq.:

H. McALLISTER, ESQ.—You are hereby commanded
to apply to the United States Supreme Court for a
Writ of Error, so that we can legally proceed to the
capitol, at Sacramento, and *burn up* the new Constitution.

Given under our hand and seal, this twenty-second
day of May, A. D., 1879. NORTON I. [SEAL.]
Dei Gratia Emperor of the United States, and Protector of Mexico.

COURTESY: WELLS FARGO BANK